amicus
illustrated

MATH WORLD
MAKING
GRAPHS

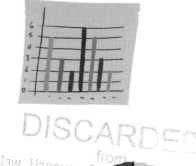

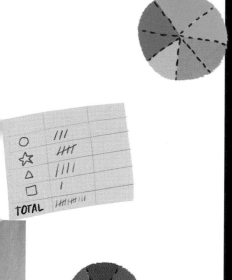

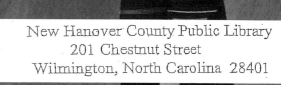

BY BRIDGET HEOS   ILLUSTRATED BY KATYA LONGHI

Amicus Illustrated is published by Amicus
P.O. Box 1329, Mankato, MN 56002
www.amicuspublishing.us

Editor: Rebecca Glaser
Designer: Kathleen Petelinsek

Library of Congress Cataloging-in-Publication Data
Heos, Bridget, author.
 Making graphs / by Bridget Heos ; illustrated by Katya Longhi.
   pages cm. — (Math world)
 Summary: "A class is learning a lesson on making graphs and
interpreting data, and the class clown, Logan, has some off-the-
wall answers to his classmates' surveys"— Provided by publisher.
 Audience: K to grade 3.
 Includes index.
 ISBN 978-1-60753-463-1 (library binding) —
 ISBN 978-1-60753-678-9 (ebook)
 1. Graphic methods—Juvenile literature. 2. Mathematics—Graphic
methods—Juvenile literature. 3. Mathematics—Charts, diagrams, etc—
Juvenile literature. I. Longhi, Katya, illustrator. II. Title.
 QA90.H36 2015
 511.5—dc23   2013034701

Printed in the United States of America at Corporate Graphics
in North Mankato, Minnesota.

10 9 8 7 6 5 4 3 2 1

ABOUT THE AUTHOR

Bridget Heos is the author of more than
60 books for kids and teens, including many
books for Amicus Illustrated, and her recent
picture book *Mustache Baby* (Houghton
Mifflin Harcourt, 2013). She lives in Kansas City
with her husband and four children. Visit her
on the Web at www.authorbridgetheos.com.

ABOUT THE ILLUSTRATOR

Katya Longhi was born in southern Italy. She
studied illustration at the Nemo NT Academy
of Digital Arts in Florence. She loves to create
dream worlds in her illustrations. She currently
lives in northern Italy with her Prince Charming.

Who is your favorite super hero? Your answer is *data*. Data means information. You can organize data by making a graph. That's what our class is doing today!

1. GATHER DATA
2. ORGANIZE THE DATA
3. INTERPRET THE DATA

LOGAN

JOSIAH

GRACE♡

TIANA

We gather data by taking surveys. A survey is when you ask many people the same question.

Josiah asks, "What's your favorite sport?"

Grace asks, "What's your favorite ice cream? Tiana, what's your question?"

I ask, "What is your favorite lunch?"

And Logan asks, "How smelly are the socks you're wearing right now?"

We each ask at least 10 people our question.

The teacher makes Logan change his question because it is too hard to measure. (Plus it was too gross!) "Okay," Logan says. "My new question is: Who is your favorite Mexican pro wrestler?"

Josiah finishes his survey first. Here are his answers:

WHAT IS YOUR FAVORITE SPORT?

- SOCCER
- BASKETBALL
- SOCCER
- SOCCER
- FOOTBALL
- GYMNASTICS
- FOOTBALL
- SOCCER
- SOCCER
- GYMNASTICS
- BASKETBALL
- GYMNASTICS
- ALLIGATOR WRESTLING

That's his data. Next, Josiah makes a tally chart. He draws a line, or tally mark, for each kid who said that sport. Then he organizes the data in order of the most popular to least popular.

Now, Josiah interprets the data. That means he says what he learned from it.

JOSIAH SPORT	TALLY	NUMBER
SOCCER	ΗΗ	5
GYMNASTICS	///	3
BASKETBALL	//	2
FOOTBALL	//	2
ALLIGATOR WRESTLING	/	1
TOTAL	ΗΗ ΗΗ ///	13

"I learned that soccer is the most popular. Gymnastics is second. Basketball is tied with football. One person said alligator wrestling. It was Logan," says Josiah.

Grace finished her ice cream
survey next. She wrote her data like this:

WHAT IS YOUR FAVORITE ICE CREAM? ♥

MICHAEL ⟶ VANILLA
ETHAN ⟶ MINT CHOCOLATE CHIP
ADDISON ⟶ VANILLA
JOSHUA ⟶ COOKIES AND CREAM
TEACHER ⟶ CHOCOLATE
AVA ⟶ CHOCOLATE
SOPHIA ⟶ COOKIES AND CREAM
TIANA ⟶ VANILLA
HUNTER ⟶ CHOCOLATE
JAYDEN ⟶ MINT CHOCOLATE CHIP
ALYSSA ⟶ VANILLA
ALEXIS ⟶ VANILLA
LOGAN ⟶ CHOCOLATE COVERED BACON

Grace organized her data in a bar graph.
She wrote the flavors on the bottom of the graph.
For each answer, she filled one square going up.

FAVORITE ICE CREAM FLAVORS

| | VANILLA | CHOCOLATE | COOKIES AND CREAM | MINT CHOCOLATE CHIP | CHOCOLATE COVERED BACON |

Then Grace interpreted her data for the class.

"Vanilla is the favorite kind (of course)! Chocolate is next. They also like cookies and cream and mint chocolate chip. Logan said the bacon one," Grace explained.

Charlie asked the same ice cream question. So Grace and Charlie combine their data. They make sure they don't count anyone's answer twice. Then they make a picture graph. Each picture represents one kid's answer.

After combining all their data, vanilla is still the most popular!

FAVORITE ICE CREAM FLAVOR

My survey answers looked like this.

WHAT'S YOUR FAVORITE SCHOOL LUNCH?

BURRITOS – 2

SLOPPY JOES – 3

PIZZA – 2

FRENCH TOAST STICKS – 1

SPAGHETTI AND COW EYE BALLS – 1

"Logan, that's not even a real lunch!" I say.
Spaghetti and cow eyeballs doesn't count. But
the lunch bell rings before I can ask someone else.

"Logan, what are you eating?" I ask.

He says, "My favorite: Spaghetti and cow eyeballs!"

Hmm . . . looks like my data might be right after all.

After lunch, I make a pie graph and interpret the data. I divide a circle (the pie) into 10 pieces. I fill in one piece of pie for each answer.

FAVORITE SCHOOL LUNCH

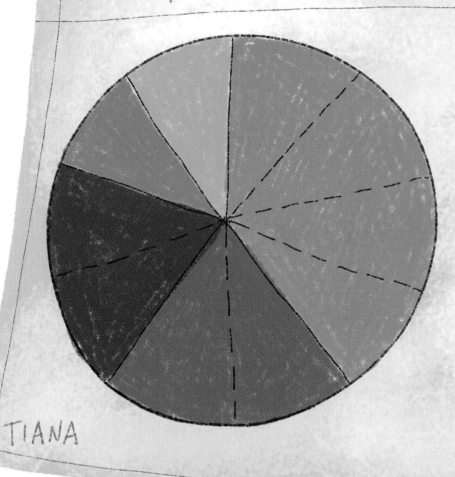

- ■ SLOPPY JOES
- ■ PIZZA
- ■ BURRITOS
- ■ FRENCH TOAST STICKS
- ■ SPAGHETTI AND ~~COW EYEBALLS~~ MEATBALLS

TIANA

"Tiana, what did you learn from your pie graph?" the teacher asks.

"Well, here's what I interpreted from my data. The most popular lunch is sloppy joes. After that, pizza and burritos are tied. And if Logan ever invites me over, I need to bring my own lunch!"

GLOSSARY

bar graph A chart that compares data by the lengths of rectangular bars.

data Information or facts.

graph A visual tool used to organize and show data.

interpret To determine what data means.

picture graph A chart that compares information by using symbols.

pie graph A chart that compares information by dividing a circle into sections.

survey A question or questions asked of many people to gather data.

tally A way to record data where you mark one line for each answer, with a diagonal line when you get to five.

READ MORE

Cocca, Lisa Colozza. **Pie Graphs**. Ann Arbor, Mich.: Cherry Lake Pub., 2013.

Loughran, Donna. **Toy Tally: How Many Toys Are There?** Chicago: Norwood House Press, 2013.

Nelson, Robin. **Let's Make a Bar Graph.** First Step Nonfiction. Minneapolis: Lerner Publications Co, 2013.

Taylor-Butler, Christine. **Understanding Charts and Graphs**. New York: Children's Press, 2012.

WEBSITES

BrainPOP Jr. | Tally Charts and Bar Graphs
http://www.brainpopjr.com/math/data/tallychartsandbargraphs/
Watch a movie about making graphs.

Create a Graph
http://nces.ed.gov/nceskids/createagraph/default.aspx
Use this interactive tool from the National Center of Education Statistics to create different types of graphs.

Math Games for Kids. Cyberchase | PBS Kids
http://pbskids.org/cyberchase/math-games/bugs-in-the-system/
Catch the bugs and make a bar graph in this PBSKids game.

Every effort has been made to ensure that these websites are appropriate for children. However, because of the nature of the Internet, it is impossible to guarantee that these sites will remain active indefinitely or that their contents will not be altered.

ML   11-14